Credit – Lit

Credit 101 for Teens

You Have This Credit Thing

Dionne Perry

Instill Publishing
Atlanta, GA

Instill Publications
2480 Briarcliff RD NE Ste 106
Box 109
Atlanta, GA 30329
www.instillpublishing.com

Cover and interior design: Anita Jones anotherjones.com

ISBN 978-1-7359470-0-6 print
ISBN 978-1-7359470-1-3 ebook

Publisher's Cataloging-In-Publication Data
(Prepared by The Donohue Group, Inc.)

Names: Perry, Dionne, author.
Title: Credit-lit : credit 101 for teens : you have this credit thing / Dionne Perry.
Other Titles: Credit lit
Description: Atlanta, GA : Instill Publishing, [2021] | Interest age level: Teens to
    young adults. | Includes bibliographical references and index. | Summary: " ...
    encourages [teens] to make GREAT financial decisions. Credit scores impact
    every financial decision. Therefore, it's important for teens to understand the
    positive and negative impacts regarding credit scores and the credit process"
    --Provided by publisher.
Identifiers: ISBN 9781735947006 (print) | ISBN 9781735947013 (ebook)
Subjects: LCSH: Credit. | Credit analysis. | Teenagers--Finance, Personal.
Classification: LCC HG3701 .P47 2021 (print) | LCC HG3701 (ebook) | DDC
    332.7083--dc23

Printed in the United States of America

This book is dedicated to the SPECIAL young people in my LIFE.

Diquan Perry, Lavelle Perry, Derek Martin, Davante James, Emry-Rae Joseph, Matthew Glasco, Ricardo Simmons, Peyton Young, Samantha Andrews, Savannah Davis, Summer Davis, Gabriel Andrews, Greyson Andrews, Taylor Rose Jordan, Zane Campbell and Zion Campbell.

As YEARS pass by, I hope you know how much you mean to ME.

About the Author & Speaker

Dionne Perry, a board-certified Credit Consultant, delivers the goods on credit, giving young people exactly what they need to make it in this economy.

With a master's degree in Human Resources a bachelor's degree in Education, Training, and Development plus experience as a licensed mortgage broker, Perry is uniquely qualified to educate young people and adults on the importance of maintaining a good credit score. Over the past twenty-five years, she's dedicated time and effort to doing exactly that!

Perry writes and speaks on the subject of credit and all its forms. As a Credit-Litologist, she can be heard on podcasts and at virtual and in-person events at schools, libraries, organizations, and businesses.

www.instillpublishing.com
www.Credit-Lit.com

Why this book – Why Now!

Credit-Lit, an inspiring and informative book will engage children of all ages and encourage them to make GREAT financial decisions.

I wrote Credit-Lit because I want to impart to young people early, the importance of having and maintaining a good credit score. I want to help young people avoid some pitfalls that many adults fall into by providing this information in an easily digestible format.

Credit scores impact every financial decision. Therefore, it's important for children of all ages to understand the positive and negative impacts regarding credit scores.

This book's purpose is to inspire teens to make great financial decisions when applying and repaying creditors now and into their adult years.

We are here to help ask the questions many teens have.

Dionne Perry provides the answers.

AND there is even more information on the website
www.Credit-Lit.com

What Is Credit?

Credit means being able to borrow money to purchase goods & services when you may not have the cash to cover the cost at that moment.

Credit is considered a loan with the understanding that the monetary balance will be paid back in agreement with the loan agreement set up by the lender (i.e., person, bank, or company) you obtain the line of credit from. This is also known as the creditor.

A line of credit is the amount of money a financial institution, like a bank or company, has agreed to lend you.

Whether or not you are granted credit is based upon your past history with borrowing and repaying creditors. Are you trustworthy? If you are issued a line of credit, will you pay the loan back timely?

How Do You Apply for Credit?

To apply for a line of credit you must be at least 18 years old and have enough income received on a regular basis (i.e. monthly) from an employer or your business.

There are different ways you can apply for credit and there are different reasons you need credit. Here is a list of just a few that might be needed as you finish high school.

- Auto Loans
- Credit Cards
- Mortgage Loans
- Student Loans

When borrowing money you don't just pay the original loan amount back, you also pay the interest. For example, if you apply for a line of credit to purchase a new laptop, you're responsible to pay the initial purchase price (cost of the laptop) and the interest or rent on the money you borrowed to purchase the laptop.

4

Credit Guidelines

Different creditors may have different guidelines based on their specific company needs. But one thing all creditors have in common is that they want:

1. The borrower to pay the agreed upon payments on time.

2. If the borrower doesn't pay the agreed upon payments on time, the lender will report a late payment on the borrower's credit report.

Credit Score

A credit score is a number that lenders use to help them decide how likely it is that they will be repaid in a timely manner.

Value Your Credit Score!

Your Credit Score Impacts Everything.

Credit Includes Making a Plan

At the time of purchase, you do not have to pay the balance (the whole amount) of whatever **goods (i.e. laptop, automobile, home, cell phone)** or services you acquire. But you ARE responsible to repay the loan amount over time.

Before you can purchase an item or service through taking out a line of credit, you have to have an agreement that tells you how and when you have to pay back the loan. This is known as a payment plan/agreement. It tells you very specifically how you are to pay and by what date.

Credit Inquiries

When applying for credit (i.e. credit cards, auto loans, mortgages) lenders will review your credit report in order to make a decision about whether they should approve or deny your request. This is considered a hard credit inquiry.

Hard inquiries occur when you've applied for credit and the lender reviews your credit report to determine your credit worthiness. A hard inquiry can potentially effect your credit scores if you allow lenders to pull your credit frequently in order to obtain a small discount towards a small purchase.

A soft inquiry occurs when you check your credit score or a lender checks your credit score for a preapproval offer. Soft inquiries do not impact your credit scores.

Don't just allow any creditor or lender to check your credit in order to obtain a small discount on a small purchase.

Different Types of Credit

Revolving Credit:

Revolving credit is a type of credit that does not have a fixed number of payments. For example, credit card accounts are considered revolving credit. You can continue to make purchases while you pay on the balances.

Installment Credit:

Installment credit is a type of agreement or contract which involves a loan that is repaid over certain amount of time with a set number of scheduled payments. For example, a car loan considered installment credit. It's just for one purchase at a time.

Open Credit:

Open credit is a pre-approved loan between a lender and a borrower. Open credit usually allows a borrower to make repeated withdrawals up to a certain limit. A personal loan is an example of open credit.

We will talk more about the types of companies that determine your credit score. But for now, the higher the number the better – the more credit-worthy you are. The number is very important as you move through different times in your life.

Your credit score is the most important number in your life.

More important than the date you were born, graduate, or wedding date.

So now my teacher is talking about Credit Agencies.
What are they for?
Why do we need three?
Do they help us?

The Different Credit Agencies
The Big Three

In the United States, there are three credit agencies (sometimes referred to as Credit Bureaus) that are used to keep track of a customer's repayment history data. These agencies are Equifax, Experian, and TransUnion.

These companies compete with one another for the ability to access your repayment history, update, and capture all of your purchasing information. The information that is retrieved is basically the same though there are slight differences.

Let's take a closer look!

EQUIFAX

Equifax uses a base scale number ranges between 280-850. The higher your Equifax score, the better your credit profile will be as you're marked as a low risk for creditors. They are far more likely to lend to you if your score is high. The higher your credit score, the less you're looked at as a credit risk. Based in Atlanta, GA.

Website: www.equifax.com

TRANSUNION

TransUnion is the smallest of The Big Three. However, this doesn't mean TransUnion is not equally as important as the bigger two. TransUnion uses VantageScore to calculate your score based on your credit and financial history. The VantageScore can range from 300-850. Headquartered in Chicago, Illinois.

Website: www.transunion.com

EXPERIAN

The only one of The Big Three that is not head-quartered in the United States, Experian is based in Dublin, Ireland. Though they are not based in America, Experian is a multi-national company that collects information from more than a billion people world-wide. This number includes over twenty-five million consumers and businesses in the US. Experian scores are based on a scale ranging from 300-850. With Experian, a score of 700 or above is considered good.

Website: www.experian.com

How Your Score Is Calculated

In order to calculate your credit score, creditors often use the Fair, Isaac, and Company (FICO) score. This score is based upon the information gathered from each of the Big Three agencies. Once the information is retrieved, the following is the formula percentage of each component:

- 35% Payment History
- 30% Current loan and Credit Card debt
- 15% Length of Credit History
- 10% Types of Credit
- 10% New Credit

FICO scores are between 300-850. In order to be considered to have good credit using your FICO score, you would need at least a 670. A score of 700 or above is generally considered very good. A score of 800 or above is considered exceptional.

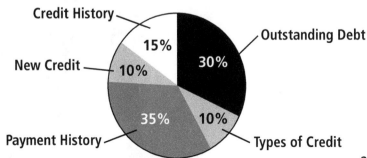

Finding Your Credit Score

Your credit score should **NEVER** be a mystery to you. You are entitled to a free complete copy (including creditor details) of your credit report every 12 months from the three credit agencies.

How can I get a
low number on my
credit score?

The Importance of Making Payments on Time

When it comes to accruing and maintaining good credit, making payments on time is critical!

When you make your payments on time, this shows potential creditors that you are a trustworthy customer. However, late payments create derogatory (negative) marks on your credit. Each derogatory mark that you receive lowers your credit score. Late payments reported to credit agencies can drop your score 50 points or more. This can impact you greatly, dropping a GREAT score down to GOOD and a GOOD score into the BAD score category.

These problems will only be made worse if your late payments are sent to a collection agency. If the account is eventually forwarded to a collection agency you will incur additional fees and the collection account will impact your score.

So, if I have a low credit score, what happens when I want to purchase something big?

Good vs. bad credit

If you are irresponsible with your credit, your low credit score can control the interest rates and or fees you pay when you purchase an item (laptop, cell phone, car, home, etc.)

Good credit is not hard to achieve if you are responsible. However, a bad credit score can limit your financial goals and impact your financial decisions for 7 years.

Length of Time Negative Marks Stay on Credit Reports

Ever heard of the saying '*Out of sight, out of mind*'? Well, that doesn't apply when it comes to your credit. Just because you break a promise arrangement or decide not to pay a bill doesn't mean that it's not still due.

Furthermore, if the outstanding balance does result in a negative mark on your credit report, that negative remark remains on your credit report for 7 years from the last payment activity date (i.e. the last date you made a payment on the account). YEARS. Truly let that sink in. We are not talking about a few weeks, or months. All it takes is one late payment to lower your score drastically for years into the future.

You are the only person who has control of your credit score. You control the credit you apply for and how you repay the loan.

Impact of Negative Credit Score

There is no way around it, having a low credit score is a headache that is extremely difficult to overcome. Negative marks (i.e., late payments, collection) on your credit has the ability to drop your score down 50 points or more per account.

Not only will you need to pay outstanding balances that caused the negative marks (which now probably include multiple late fees, high interest rates, and fines), your low credit score also takes away a lot of your buying options.

When it comes to the type of car you drive, the amount of money banks are willing to lend to you, and even the neighborhood and home you live in; all of these things can be impacted because of a low credit score.

Let's compare an example of the interest rate on a car for someone with good credit versus a person with a bad score.

The higher the credit score the less interest you repay to the lender/creditor.

Credit Score Ranges

350 to 500: Applicants will not likely be approved for credit.

500 to 600: Applicants may be approved for some credit; however, the interest rates may be unfavorable and require the applicant to make a large down payment.

601 to 660: Applicants may be approved for credit; however, the interest rate may be high.

661 to 780: Applicants likely to be approved for credit at competitive interest rates.

781 to 850: Applicants most likely to be approved and receive the best interest rates and most favorable loan terms. No down payment usually required.

High Credit Scores equals lower payments.

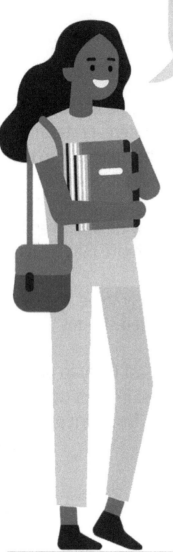

IMPACTS OF A HIGH CREDIT SCORE VERSUS LOW CREDIT SCORE

Credit Score	New Car Annual Percentage Rate	Loan Term
750 & Higher	1.99 APR	5 years
749 to 699	2.99 APR	5 years
698 to 648	4.99 APR	5 years
647 to 597	6.99 APR	5 years
596 to 546	11.99 APR	5 years
546 & Lower	Loan Application Denied	N/A

For example, if you purchase a new car for $20,000 and your credit score is 750 or higher, your monthly car pay amount is $350.47 versus if your credit score was 596, your monthly car payment amount is $444.79.

By having a higher credit score you save $94.32 a month!

The estimated car payment was based on the APR listed in the above chart.

The Perks of Having a High Credit Score

You are now seeing that a good credit score is a big deal. There are major advantages that come with taking your credit seriously.

Not only is a high score extremely impressive to creditors, having a high credit score can come with many rewards.

Having a high credit score can save you thousands by avoiding high interest rates, late fees, and penalties. Here is a list of perks just waiting for you.

- Lower interest rates
- Avoid security deposits for apartments or loans
- The ability to purchase what you want from lenders (i.e., banks, credit unions, creditors) without paying a high interest rate or a deposit.

- Lower interest rates when purchasing cell phones and other high-priced electronics (i.e., laptops, digital cameras, etc.)
- Lower monthly loan payments
- Easier to get approved for loans or line of credit
- Avoid security deposit for utilities (i.e., electricity, cable, water)

How Your Credit Score Can Impact Your Dream Job

Did you know? Sometimes employers will also pull your credit report as a way to determine whether you'd be a reliable employee. That may seem well and good, but it can also have an adverse impact. Negative items (i.e., late payments, collection) may be reported to all three of the major agencies. If you have several late payments reported to the credit agencies, the late payments will lower your credit score. The employer may take into consideration how responsible you may be as their employee.

Why is it so important to protect your personal credit file?

It's especially important to actively monitor your personal credit file once you become an adult. Unfortunately, someone can steal your identity and purchase items or obtain a line of credit using your social security number.

Remember these key points:
Value Your Credit Score!

Your Credit Score impacts everything.

Don't just allow any creditor or lender to check your credit in order to obtain a small discount on a purchase.

Safeguard your identify while online! Don't enter your personal information (i.e., date of birth, social security number, and home address) when browsing or surfing online.

Every want is not a need. Make sure you can afford the goods (i.e., laptop, cell phone, auto-mobile, etc.) or services before applying for a line of credit.

You are the only person who has control of your credit score. You control the credit you apply for and how you repay the loan agreement.

Your credit score is the most important number in your life. More important than the date you were born, graduate, or wedding date.

Credit impacts everything.

Now that you have a better understanding of credit and how it works, you will be able to make smarter, sounder financial decisions as you become an adult.

Congratulations, you're officially Credit-Lit!

Want to know more? Want help
with a credit issue?

Follow Credit-Lit on these social media platforms
for daily posts, freebies, new releases, and
much more.

Website: www.Credit-Lit.com

Facebook: https://www.facebook.com/Credit-Lit

Instagram: https://www.instagram.com/credit.lit/

Twitter: https://twitter.com/litcredit

Pinterest: https://www.pinterest.com/
         instillpublishingmarketing

Tumblr: https://www.tumblr.com/blog/credit-lit

Glossary

Annual Percentage Rate (APR): The annual percentage rate you pay back for the entire year.

Bank: A financial institution that loans consumers money via a repayment plan.

Card issuer: A financial institution, bank, credit union or company that issues a line of credit to a consumer using a plastic card.

Cardholder: A cardholder is an individual to whom a business issued a card or who is authorized to use an issued card.

Collection: Collection is an effort by a collections department or agency to get a past-due debt repaid. Creditors usually report collection debts to credit agencies. Collection debts can impact your ability to borrow at reasonable rates.

Creditor: A creditor is a person, organization or company that lends you money.

Consumer Financial Protection Bureau: The Consumer Financial Protection Bureau, or CFPB, is a federal agency charged with being a watchdog for consumer financial products, such as credit cards, payday loans, mortgages, and student loans.

Credit History: Credit history is the record of use of debt. The three major credit agencies track individuals' credit histories and compile them into credit reports. Lenders (i.e. banks, credit unions, etc.) use credit histories to decide whether to provide customers with credit, and on what terms.

Credit Inquiry: A credit inquiry is created when a lender pulls your credit record.

Credit Limit: A credit limit is the maximum amount of money the lender is willing to loan a consumer.

Credit Report: A credit report is an individual compilation of your credit history. The credit report details your history of borrowing, payment behavior and credit inquiries. Credit reports are viewed by lenders in deciding whether to extend credit to you and on what terms.

Credit Freeze: A credit freeze is a service available to consumers through the credit agencies in which consumers can freeze their credit, preventing new accounts from being opened or someone pulling your credit report without your consent. Credit freeze is a useful tool if someone steals your identify.

Credit Score: A credit score is a three-digit number that summarizes how well you repay debt to lenders.

The higher the credit score number, the better. Individuals with high credit scores can qualify for larger loans with lower interest rates. Individuals with low credit scores may be turned down for credit or approved for a smaller amount with high interest rates.

Credit Reporting Agency (CRA): A credit reporting agency (CRA) is a company that tracks and sells your credit history to lenders.

Credit Utilization Ratio: A credit utilization ratio is used in the calculation of your credit scores. It compares the amount of credit you are using to the total credit available to you.

Credit Union: A credit union is a member-owned financial institution controlled by its members and operated on the principle of people helping people, usually providing its members financial services (i.e. loans, credit) at very competitive rates.

Credit Monitoring Service: A credit monitoring service monitors your payment history and notifies you of suspicious or out of pattern activity on your credit report. Credit monitoring services charge a fee to monitor your credit.

Hard Inquiry: A hard inquiry occurs when you've applied for credit and the lender or creditor pulls your credit score for review to determine your credit worthiness.

Identity Theft: Identity theft is the deliberate use of someone else's identity, usually as a method to gain a financial advantage or obtain credit and other benefits in the other person's name.

Installment Credit: Installment credit is a type of agreement or contract that involves a loan to be repaid over a certain amount of time with a set number of scheduled payments. For example, car loans are considered installment credit.

Interest Rate: The rate a bank or lender charges you to borrow its money. The higher your credit score, the lower your interest rate. The lower your credit score, the higher your interest rate. If your credit score is low, the bank or lender will charge you more money to borrow their money.

Late Payment Fee: A late payment fee is charged to a borrower who misses paying their minimum payment by the payment due date. In order to avoid late fees, always pay at least the minimum amount by the due date. Late payments will affect your credit score.

Lender: A lender is a person, organization or company that lends you money.

Line of Credit: A line of credit is the amount of money a financial institution like a bank or company has agreed to lend you.

Open Credit: Open Credit is a pre-approved loan between a lender and a borrower. Open credit usually allows a borrower to make repeated withdrawals up to a certain limit.

Revolving Credit: Revolving Credit is a type of credit that does not have a fixed number of payments, in contrast to installment credit. For example, credit cards are considered revolving credit.

Social Security Number: A Social Security number is a nine-digit number assigned to citizens, permanent residents, and temporary (working) residents. When applying for credit, you have to provide your Social Security number.

Soft Inquiry: A soft inquiry occurs when you check your credit score or a lender checks your credit score for a preapproval offer. Soft inquires do not impact your credit scores.

Join us on the Credit-Lit journey.

Email us at ambassador@Credit-Lit.com and we will send you the steps to benefits and how to get started.

Credit-Lit Ambassador Programs

Join Our Credit-Lit Teen Ambassador Program

This teen program, available for teens ages 13-19, offers an exciting opportunity to be a part of a movement empowering others.

Credit-Lit ambassadors are motivated and diverse students from across the United States who are committed to inspiring one another to make great financial decisions. They represent the distinct ideas, opinions and attitudes, knowledge, and actions of today's teen as a collective body. The Credit-Lit ambassador strives to bring awareness of the importance of maintaining a good credit score as an adult.

Sign up now to learn more about the benefits!

Join Our Credit-Lit Adult Ambassador Program

This adult program, available to educators, community activists, parents, and financial advisors offers an exciting opportunity to be a part of a movement empowering teens.

Join this program and work with us on the Credit-Lit campaign to help educate teens on how the credit score process works.